Real Estate Book on Managing Rental Properties

A Comprehensive Guide to Successful Rental Property Management

REAL ESTATE BOOK ON MANAGING RENTAL PROPERTIES

First edition. December 4, 2023.

ISBN: 979-8215519585

Written by Andan Maharma.

Table of Contents

Adnan Maharma

Chapter One: Introduction

Welcome to the world of real estate investment and property management! Whether you are a seasoned investor or a novice looking to venture into the lucrative realm of rental properties, this book aims to equip you with the knowledge and tools necessary for successful rental property management.

Section 1: Importance of Effective Rental Property Management

Owning rental properties can be a rewarding and profitable venture, providing a steady stream of passive income and the potential for long-term wealth accumulation. However, it is essential to recognize that successful rental property management is far more than just buying a property and collecting rent. The significance of effective management cannot be overstated, and it can spell the difference between a prosperous investment and a costly headache.

Effective property management involves a wide array of responsibilities, including property maintenance, tenant relations, legal compliance, financial management, and marketing. Neglecting any of these aspects can lead to numerous challenges, such as high tenant turnover, property damage, legal disputes, and financial losses. On the other hand, implementing a well-thought-out management strategy can help maximize property value, attract reliable tenants, ensure a consistent cash flow, and minimize potential risks.

Throughout this book, we will explore the essential elements of rental property management, offering insights, tips, and best practices to help you navigate the real estate market successfully.

Section 2: Setting Realistic Goals for Property Investment

Before diving headfirst into the rental property market, it is crucial to establish realistic and achievable investment goals. Your goals will shape your entire property management approach, influencing decisions regarding property type, location, budgeting, and more.

As an investor, take some time for self-reflection and ask yourself the following questions:

What is my motivation for investing in rental properties? Are you seeking steady cash flow, long-term appreciation, or both?

What level of involvement am I willing to commit to property management? Are you planning to manage the property yourself, or will you hire a professional property management company?

What is my budget for investment? Consider not only the property's purchase price but also ongoing expenses like maintenance, property taxes, insurance, and marketing.

How much risk am I willing to tolerate? Different types of properties and locations come with varying levels of risk and potential returns.

What is my target market? Define the type of tenants you wish to attract and tailor your property choices accordingly.

By setting clear and attainable goals, you can focus your efforts and resources effectively, making smarter decisions throughout your property investment journey.

In the following chapters, we will delve deeper into each aspect of rental property management, offering actionable advice and insights from experienced investors and property managers. Remember, success in this field requires continuous learning and adaptation to the ever-changing dynamics of the real estate market.

So, let's embark on this journey together and unlock the secrets to effective rental property management, turning your investment endeavors into a prosperous and rewarding experience. Get ready to take the first steps towards becoming a successful rental property manager!

Chapter Two: Understanding the Rental Market

Section 1: Researching Local Rental Market Trends

To effectively manage rental properties, it is vital to have a comprehensive understanding of the local rental market. Market dynamics can vary significantly from one area to another, and staying informed about current trends and developments will give you a competitive edge in making informed decisions.

Conducting Market Research: Begin by conducting thorough market research on the specific location where your rental property is situated or where you intend to invest. Rely on a combination of online resources, government data, and local property management companies to gather relevant information. Look into historical and current rental rates, vacancy rates, and the overall demand for rental properties in the area.

Analyzing Rental Rates: Rental rates play a crucial role in attracting tenants and maximizing your rental income. Compare rental rates for properties similar to yours in the neighborhood. Take into account factors such as property size, location, amenities, and condition. Strive to strike the right balance between offering competitive rates and ensuring your property's profitability.

Understanding Vacancy Rates: High vacancy rates could indicate an oversaturated rental market or potential issues with the property itself. It is essential to investigate the reasons behind vacancies and take proactive steps to address them. Regularly monitoring vacancy rates will help you detect any trends and make necessary adjustments to your rental strategy.

Examining Market Trends: The rental market is influenced by various economic and demographic factors. Stay updated with local economic trends, such as job growth, industry development, and population changes. These factors can significantly impact the demand for rental properties in the area. Additionally, consider factors like new construction projects, zoning changes, and infrastructure developments that might affect the rental landscape.

Engaging with Real Estate Professionals: Networking with local real estate agents, property managers, and industry experts can provide valuable insights into the current market conditions and future projections. These professionals have firsthand experience dealing with rental properties in the area and can offer advice on property investment, pricing, and market trends.

Understanding Legal and Regulatory Aspects: It is crucial to familiarize yourself with local rental laws, tenant rights, and landlord responsibilities. Complying with legal requirements not only protects your interests as a landlord but also ensures a positive tenant experience, reducing the risk of legal disputes.

Section 2: Identifying Target Demographics and Tenants

Understanding your target demographic is a crucial aspect of successful rental property management. Different properties attract different types of tenants, and tailoring your property to meet their needs will enhance its appeal and reduce vacancies.

Analyzing Demographics: Study the demographics of the area surrounding your rental property. Consider factors such as age groups, income levels, and family sizes. This information will help you determine the most suitable property features and amenities for your target tenants. For example, properties located near universities might be appealing to students, while areas with growing families may require larger units with safe outdoor spaces.

Evaluating Local Amenities: The proximity of your property to essential amenities plays a significant role in attracting tenants. Tenants often prioritize access to schools, hospitals, public transportation, shopping centers, and recreational facilities. Evaluating the availability and quality of these amenities in the neighborhood will help you market your property effectively.

Catering to Specific Tenant Needs: Depending on the location, you may find that certain amenities or property features are more desirable to tenants. For example, properties located in vibrant urban areas might attract young professionals who value proximity to entertainment and dining options. On the other hand, properties in family-oriented neighborhoods may require larger units with secure outdoor spaces for children to play.

Identifying Niche Markets: In some cases, targeting a specific niche market can be advantageous. By identifying niche markets, you can create a unique selling point for your rental property. For instance, properties designed for senior citizens might offer accessibility features and proximity to healthcare facilities. Properties that welcome pet owners might have pet-friendly amenities and nearby parks.

Understanding Tenant Preferences: To improve tenant satisfaction and retention, consider conducting surveys or engaging in direct conversations with your existing tenants. Understanding their preferences, concerns, and suggestions will help you make improvements that enhance the overall tenant experience. Happy tenants are more likely to renew their leases and recommend your property to others, contributing to your long-term success as a rental property manager.

By carefully researching the rental market and identifying your target demographics, you can position your rental property for success. Keep in mind that the rental market is dynamic, and regular assessments will help you adapt to changing trends, ensuring your property remains competitive and profitable in the long run. As you delve deeper into the world of rental property management, remember that knowledge, preparation, and a tenant-centric approach are key ingredients for success in this rewarding field.

Chapter Three: Financial Planning for Real Estate Investment

Section 1: Creating a Budget and Financial Forecast

Effective financial planning is at the heart of successful real estate investment. Before acquiring a rental property, it is essential to create a comprehensive budget and financial forecast that outlines all the expenses and potential income associated with the investment.

Assessing Initial Costs: Start by identifying all the upfront costs involved in purchasing the rental property. This includes the down payment, closing costs, property appraisal fees, and any necessary renovations or repairs before making the property rent-ready.

Calculating Operating Expenses: Operating expenses are ongoing costs associated with managing the rental property. They typically include property taxes, insurance premiums, utilities (if not passed on to tenants), property management fees (if applicable), regular maintenance, and potential homeowner association fees.

Accounting for Vacancy and Turnover: Anticipate periods when your property might be vacant between tenants or when tenants are transitioning. Budgeting for vacancy and turnover costs will help you avoid cash flow disruptions during these periods.

Factoring in Capital Expenditures: Over time, certain components of the property may require significant repairs or replacements. These capital expenditures might include roof repairs, HVAC system replacements, or major appliance upgrades. Setting aside funds for future capital expenditures will ensure you're prepared for these larger expenses when they arise.

Estimating Rental Income: Forecast the rental income based on current market rental rates and demand for properties similar to yours in the area. Be realistic with your estimates to avoid potential disappointments and ensure you can cover your expenses even during times of fluctuating rental demand.

Cash Flow Analysis: Analyze the expected cash flow of the rental property by deducting all expenses from the projected rental income. A positive cash flow indicates that your property generates more income than it costs to operate, which is generally a desirable outcome.

Section 2: Financing Options for Rental Properties

After creating a detailed budget and financial forecast, the next crucial step is to explore financing options for acquiring the rental property. There are several common financing methods to consider:

Conventional Mortgage: A conventional mortgage is a popular financing option for rental properties. It typically requires a down payment of 20% or more and is obtained through a bank or mortgage lender. Interest rates and terms may vary, so it's essential to shop around for the best rates and conditions.

Government-Backed Loans: Government-backed loans, such as FHA (Federal Housing Administration) or VA (Veterans Affairs) loans, can be an attractive option for first-time investors or individuals who qualify for these programs. These loans often offer lower down payment requirements and more lenient credit qualifications.

Private Lenders: Private lenders, such as individuals or private investment firms, can provide alternative financing options. Private loans may be more flexible in terms of eligibility criteria and repayment terms, but they often come with higher interest rates.

Seller Financing: In some cases, sellers may be willing to finance a portion of the property's purchase price. This arrangement involves the buyer making payments directly to the seller over an agreed-upon period, avoiding the need for a traditional mortgage.

Real Estate Investment Partnerships: Joining forces with other investors through real estate partnerships can help pool financial resources and reduce individual financial burdens. Partnerships can also provide diverse skill sets and knowledge, leading to more successful property management.

Home Equity Line of Credit (HELOC): If you already own a property with substantial equity, you may consider obtaining a HELOC to finance your rental property investment. A HELOC uses the equity in your current property as collateral for a line of credit.

Before selecting a financing option, thoroughly assess each choice's terms, interest rates, and repayment schedules. Choosing the right financing method can significantly impact the financial viability of your rental property investment.

By meticulously creating a budget and financial forecast and exploring various financing options, you will be better prepared to make informed decisions and embark on a successful and financially sound real estate investment journey. Remember that financial planning is an ongoing process, and periodic reassessment of your budget and investment strategy is crucial to adapt to changing market conditions and ensure long-term profitability.

Chapter Four: Finding Profitable Rental Properties

Section 1: Property Hunting and Due Diligence

Finding profitable rental properties requires a meticulous approach to property hunting and conducting thorough due diligence. This section will delve deeper into the essential steps that will help you identify potential rental investments and assess their viability.

Setting Investment Criteria: Take the time to define your investment criteria in detail. Consider factors such as the type of property (single-family homes, multi-unit buildings, condos, etc.), preferred locations (urban, suburban, or rural), budget constraints, and desired return on investment (ROI). Having clear and well-defined criteria will guide your search and prevent you from investing in properties that do not align with your long-term goals.

Utilizing Multiple Sources: To maximize your chances of finding the right rental property, cast a wide net when searching. Utilize various sources, including online listings, real estate agents, property auctions, local classifieds, and networking within the real estate community. Each source may offer unique opportunities, and being proactive in your search will increase the likelihood of finding the best deals.

Analyzing Neighborhoods: Thoroughly research the neighborhoods where you are considering purchasing a rental property. Look for areas with low crime rates, good school districts, access to public transportation, amenities (parks, shopping centers, restaurants), and positive economic indicators (job growth, population growth, infrastructure development). A well-chosen location can significantly influence the property's demand, potential for appreciation, and the quality of tenants you attract.

Conducting Due Diligence: Due diligence is a critical step in the property acquisition process. It involves conducting a comprehensive investigation of the property's history and current condition. Review property records, past rental income, current and potential expenses (property taxes, insurance, utilities), tax history, and any potential legal issues. Engage a qualified inspector to assess the property's physical condition, identifying any hidden problems that may impact its value or require costly repairs.

Evaluating Rental Demand: Analyze the rental demand in the area where the property is located. High rental demand indicates a favorable market for landlords, as it increases the likelihood of securing reliable tenants and maintaining low vacancy rates. Factors such as population growth, employment opportunities, and the presence of educational institutions can influence rental demand.

Market Rent Analysis: Compare the property's potential rental income to similar rental properties in the area. Research current rental rates for properties with similar features, size, and location. Analyze whether the property's rental income is competitive or can be increased over time based on market trends and tenant preferences.

Property Appreciation Potential: Consider the potential for property appreciation over time. Look into historical trends of property values in the area to assess the likelihood of your investment appreciating in value. A property that appreciates over time can significantly boost your overall return on investment.

Section 2: Evaluating Potential Rental Investments

Evaluating rental investments involves a comprehensive analysis of the financial aspects of each property to determine its potential profitability and suitability for your investment portfolio.

Cash Flow Analysis: The foundation of a profitable rental investment is positive cash flow. Calculate the property's cash flow by deducting all expenses (including mortgage, property taxes, insurance, maintenance, property management fees, and vacancies) from the expected rental income. A positive cash flow indicates that the property generates more income than it costs to operate, providing you with a consistent source of passive income.

Capitalization Rate (Cap Rate): The capitalization rate is a fundamental metric used to evaluate the profitability of a rental property. It is calculated by dividing the property's net operating income (NOI) by its current market value. A higher cap rate generally indicates a better return on investment, but it's essential to consider other factors alongside the cap rate to make an informed decision.

Return on Investment (ROI): ROI takes into account both cash flow and property appreciation over time. Calculate the ROI by considering the property's initial investment and the expected return over a specific holding period. This metric allows you to compare the potential returns of different properties and make more informed investment decisions.

Financial Projections: Create financial projections for the rental property based on historical data, market trends, and your assessment of future performance. Consider potential risks and uncertainties, such as changes in the local economy or rental market conditions, and develop contingency plans to mitigate these risks.

Assessing Risk: Evaluate the level of risk associated with the investment. Consider factors such as the stability of the local rental market, potential fluctuations in property values, and the property's susceptibility to natural disasters or other hazards. Understanding and managing risk are essential components of a successful rental property investment strategy.

Exit Strategy: Develop a clear exit strategy for each potential investment. Consider how you will handle the property if market conditions change, your financial goals evolve, or you encounter unexpected challenges. A well-defined exit strategy allows you to make informed decisions and pivot if necessary.

Remember, finding profitable rental properties requires patience, thorough research, and a sound financial analysis. Avoid making impulsive decisions and prioritize properties that align with your investment goals and risk tolerance. By conducting due diligence and carefully evaluating potential rental investments, you can increase the likelihood of selecting properties that provide consistent cash flow, long-term appreciation, and a successful rental property portfolio. Be willing to adapt and refine your criteria as you gain experience and knowledge in the real estate market, and always seek professional advice when needed to make well-informed investment decisions. With the right approach and strategic planning, you can build a profitable and resilient rental property portfolio that will contribute to your financial success and long-term wealth-building goals.

Chapter Five: Property Acquisition and Legal Considerations

Section 1: Navigating Real Estate Contracts and Transactions

Property acquisition involves complex legal processes and transactions that must be handled with care and attention to detail. This section will guide you through the key steps and considerations when navigating real estate contracts and transactions.

Engaging Real Estate Professionals:

When navigating real estate contracts and transactions, it is beneficial to work with experienced real estate professionals, such as a real estate agent or attorney. A real estate agent can help you find suitable properties, negotiate the purchase price, and guide you through the transaction process. An attorney can provide legal advice, review contracts, and ensure that your interests are protected throughout the transaction.

Letter of Intent (LOI):

The Letter of Intent (LOI) is a preliminary document that outlines the key terms and conditions of a potential real estate transaction. It is a non-binding agreement and serves as a starting point for negotiations between the buyer and the seller. The LOI typically includes details such as the proposed purchase price, financing arrangements, contingencies, and the expected closing date. Although the LOI is not legally binding, it sets the groundwork for drafting the formal Purchase and Sale Agreement.

Purchase and Sale Agreement:

The Purchase and Sale Agreement is a legally binding contract that outlines the specific terms and conditions of the property purchase. It is the most critical document in the transaction process. The agreement includes details such as the purchase price, the closing date, any contingencies, and specific conditions unique to the transaction. Both parties must carefully review and understand the terms before signing the agreement.

Contingencies:

Contingencies are clauses in the Purchase and Sale Agreement that allow the buyer to withdraw from the contract without penalty under specific circumstances. Common contingencies include:

- Inspection Contingency: This allows the buyer to conduct a property inspection to identify any issues or defects. If significant problems are found during the inspection, the buyer can negotiate repairs or cancel the contract.

- Financing Contingency: This allows the buyer to back out of the contract if they are unable to secure the necessary financing to purchase the property.

- Appraisal Contingency: This contingency enables the buyer to cancel the contract if the property's appraised value is lower than the agreed-upon purchase price.

Property Inspections:

A comprehensive property inspection is essential to assess the property's condition and identify any potential problems. Hire qualified inspectors to inspect the structural integrity, electrical systems, plumbing, HVAC, and any other critical aspects of the property. The inspection report will help you make informed decisions about the property and may provide leverage for negotiating repairs or adjustments to the purchase price.

Title Search and Title Insurance:

A title search is conducted to ensure that the property's title is clear of any liens, encumbrances, or legal issues. Title insurance protects both the buyer and the lender from any undiscovered title defects that may arise in the future. It provides financial compensation in case of title-related disputes.

Financing and Mortgage Agreements:

If you require financing to purchase the property, work closely with your lender to secure a mortgage that aligns with your financial needs and goals. Review the terms and conditions of the mortgage agreement, including interest rates, loan duration, and any prepayment penalties. Be prepared to provide the necessary financial documentation to the lender during the loan application process.

Section 2: Complying with Property Laws and Regulations

Landlord-Tenant Laws:

Landlord-tenant laws govern the rights and responsibilities of both landlords and tenants. These laws vary by jurisdiction but often cover issues such as lease agreements, security deposits, rent increases, eviction procedures, and tenant privacy rights. Familiarize yourself with the specific laws in your area and ensure that all interactions with tenants adhere to these regulations.

Fair Housing Laws:

Fair housing laws prohibit discrimination based on protected characteristics, such as race, color, national origin, religion, sex, disability, and familial status. It is essential to understand and comply with these laws throughout the tenant screening and selection process. Use consistent and objective criteria when evaluating potential tenants to avoid any allegations of discrimination.

Local Zoning and Property Use Regulations:

Local zoning regulations dictate how properties can be used within specific areas. Ensure that your rental property is in compliance with local zoning laws, as violating these regulations can lead to fines and legal repercussions. Additionally, be aware of any restrictions on short-term rentals or other specific property use restrictions that may apply in your area.

Building Codes and Safety Regulations:

Complying with building codes and safety regulations is crucial for maintaining a safe and habitable rental property. Ensure that the property meets all safety standards, including proper fire exits, functioning smoke detectors, and other essential safety features. Regularly inspect and maintain the property to uphold these standards.

Rent Control and Rent Increase Restrictions:

Some jurisdictions have rent control laws that limit the amount and frequency of rent increases. Research and understand the rent control regulations in your area to ensure compliance with these laws. In locations without rent control, it is essential to provide appropriate notice to tenants before implementing rent increases.

Taxation and Reporting Requirements:

Owning a rental property has tax implications, and it is crucial to comply with all tax laws and reporting requirements. Keep meticulous records of income and expenses related to the property, including maintenance costs, property taxes, insurance premiums, and other deductible expenses. Consult with a tax professional to maximize tax benefits and ensure accurate reporting.

Environmental Regulations:

Depending on the property's location and characteristics, it may be subject to specific environmental regulations. For example, properties near water bodies or wetlands may have restrictions on development or require additional environmental assessments. Be aware of any environmental regulations that may apply to your property and seek professional advice if necessary.

By navigating real estate contracts and transactions with the guidance of professionals and complying with property laws and regulations, you can protect your investment and establish a strong legal foundation for successful rental property management. Always stay informed about any changes in laws or regulations, and seek legal advice when needed to ensure compliance and minimize potential legal risks. Operating within the boundaries of the law will not only protect your interests as a landlord but also foster positive tenant relationships and contribute to the long-term success of your rental property portfolio.

Chapter Six: Preparing Your Rental Property

Section 1: Renovations, Repairs, and Upgrades

Preparing your rental property involves making necessary renovations, repairs, and upgrades to ensure it is in excellent condition and attractive to potential tenants. A well-maintained property not only enhances tenant satisfaction but also reduces the likelihood of issues and vacancies.

Assessing Property Condition: Begin by conducting a thorough assessment of the property's condition. Identify any areas that require immediate attention, such as leaking roofs, faulty plumbing, electrical issues, or structural problems. Prioritize repairs that impact the property's habitability and safety.

Repairs and Maintenance: Address all necessary repairs promptly and efficiently. Fix broken windows, doors, locks, and appliances. Ensure that plumbing fixtures and electrical systems are in good working order. Regularly inspect the property for maintenance needs, such as repainting walls, fixing leaks, and addressing pest infestations.

Safety and Compliance: Ensure that your rental property meets all safety standards and regulatory requirements. Install smoke detectors, carbon monoxide detectors, and fire extinguishers in compliance with local laws. Make sure staircases and handrails are secure and that the property has proper emergency exits.

Energy Efficiency Upgrades: Consider energy-efficient upgrades that can reduce utility costs for both you and your tenants. Install energy-efficient windows, LED lighting, programmable thermostats, and energy-efficient appliances. These upgrades can also make your property more attractive to environmentally conscious tenants.

Cosmetic Improvements: Cosmetic improvements can significantly enhance your property's appeal. Repaint the walls with a neutral and inviting color scheme. Replace worn-out flooring or carpets. Consider upgrading kitchen and bathroom fixtures to modern and functional designs. These improvements can help attract quality tenants and justify higher rental rates.

Landscaping: Maintaining the property's exterior is equally important. Ensure the lawn is well-kept and free of weeds. Trim trees and bushes, and clean up any debris or clutter in the yard. Add attractive landscaping elements, such as flowers or potted plants, to create a welcoming atmosphere.

Section 2: Attracting Quality Tenants through Curb Appeal

Curb appeal plays a crucial role in attracting quality tenants and ensuring that your rental property remains occupied. A well-maintained exterior creates a positive first impression and sets the stage for a positive tenant experience.

Exterior Maintenance: Regularly inspect the property's exterior for any signs of wear and tear. Repair or replace damaged siding, roof shingles, and gutters. Ensure that the property's facade is clean and free from mold or mildew.

Enhance Entryways: The entryway is the focal point of the property. Enhance it with a fresh coat of paint on the front door, new house numbers, and stylish outdoor lighting. Consider adding a welcome mat and potted plants to create a warm and inviting entry.

Well-Lit Exterior: Adequate outdoor lighting not only improves safety but also enhances the property's overall appeal. Install outdoor lighting fixtures along pathways, near entryways, and in the backyard. Well-lit exteriors create a sense of security for tenants.

Functional Outdoor Spaces: If the property has a backyard or patio area, ensure it is well-maintained and functional. Add outdoor furniture, such as a table and chairs or a lounge set, to showcase the potential for outdoor living and entertaining.

Clean and Tidy Common Areas: If the property includes common areas, such as hallways or shared laundry rooms, keep them clean and well-maintained. A clean and tidy environment contributes to a positive tenant experience and fosters a sense of community.

Professional Photography: When marketing your rental property, invest in professional photography to showcase its curb appeal. High-quality images capture the property's best features and attract more potential tenants.

Effective Marketing: Utilize various marketing channels to promote your rental property's curb appeal. List the property on popular rental websites, use social media to showcase photos and videos, and create eye-catching rental ads.

By focusing on renovations, repairs, and upgrades to enhance your rental property's condition and curb appeal, you can attract quality tenants and create a positive rental experience. A well-maintained property demonstrates your commitment to providing a comfortable and attractive living environment for your tenants. Remember that first impressions matter, and investing time and resources in preparing your rental property will pay off with increased tenant interest, reduced vacancies, and higher tenant satisfaction in the long run.

Chapter Seven: Setting the Right Rent
Section 1: Pricing Strategies for Maximum Profitability

Setting the right rent for your rental property is crucial to maximize profitability while remaining competitive in the market. An optimal rental price will attract quality tenants and ensure a steady stream of income for your investment.

Conduct Market Research: Begin by conducting thorough market research to understand the current rental landscape in your area. Analyze rental rates for similar properties in the neighborhood and compare them to your property's features and amenities. Online rental listings, property management companies, and real estate agents can provide valuable data for your research.

Consider Supply and Demand: Pay attention to the supply and demand dynamics in the rental market. High demand and low supply may allow you to set higher rents, while an oversaturated market may require more competitive pricing to attract tenants.

Calculate Operating Expenses: Factor in all operating expenses associated with your rental property, including property taxes, insurance, maintenance costs, property management fees (if applicable), and any utilities or services you plan to include in the rent. Subtract these expenses from the potential rental income to determine the property's net operating income (NOI).

Determine Cash Flow Goals: Decide on your cash flow goals and desired return on investment (ROI). Assess whether your rental property's potential cash flow aligns with these goals. Adjust the rent accordingly to achieve your financial objectives.

Use Pricing Strategies: Consider different pricing strategies based on market conditions and property-specific factors. For example, you may choose to price your rental slightly below market rates to attract tenants quickly or offer competitive rental incentives.

Offer Value-Added Amenities: Adding value to your rental property can justify higher rent. Consider offering desirable amenities, such as in-unit laundry, high-speed internet, covered parking, or access to shared amenities like a pool or fitness center.

Section 2: Balancing Market Rates and Property Value

Striking the right balance between market rates and your property's value is essential for setting a competitive rent that attracts quality tenants and ensures a profitable rental venture.

Evaluate Property Features: Consider the unique features and qualities of your rental property. A property with premium features, such as a great view, updated kitchen, or spacious backyard, may command a higher rent than comparable properties without these features.

Assess Property Condition: The overall condition of your rental property can influence its value and rental potential. A well-maintained property with modern upgrades is likely to justify a higher rent than a property in need of significant repairs.

Analyze Location Benefits: The location of your rental property is a critical factor in determining its value. Properties in desirable neighborhoods with access to amenities, schools, public transportation, and employment centers generally have a higher rental value.

Tenant Profile: Consider your target tenant profile when setting the rent. If your property is attractive to a specific demographic, such as young professionals or families, you can adjust the rent accordingly to accommodate their preferences and budget constraints.

Stay Competitive: While it is essential to recognize your property's value, be mindful of the local rental market's competitive rates. Setting rent significantly higher than similar properties without valid justifications may deter potential tenants and lead to extended vacancies.

Regular Rent Reviews: Regularly review the rental market and your property's performance. If market conditions change or property values increase significantly, consider adjusting the rent to align with current trends and maintain profitability.

Tenant Retention: It's often more cost-effective to retain existing tenants than to find new ones. Consider offering lease renewal incentives, providing excellent customer service, and addressing maintenance requests promptly to encourage tenant retention.

Finding the right rent requires a delicate balance between market rates, property value, and your financial goals. Regularly review and adjust the rent as needed to remain competitive and ensure that your rental property continues to attract quality tenants. A well-priced rental property will not only maximize profitability but also foster positive tenant relationships, leading to a successful and rewarding rental property management experience.

Chapter Eight: Effective Tenant Screening

Section 1: Tenant Application and Screening Process

An effective tenant screening process is crucial for selecting reliable and responsible tenants who will uphold the terms of the lease agreement and maintain the property. Proper screening minimizes the risk of potential problems and helps ensure a positive rental experience for both you and your tenants.

Create a Comprehensive Rental Application: Design a detailed rental application that collects essential information from prospective tenants. Include questions about employment history, income, rental history, references, and any additional occupants. The application should comply with fair housing laws and not request information that could lead to discrimination.

Require Supporting Documentation: Request supporting documents to verify the information provided in the application. This may include recent pay stubs, employment verification, previous landlord references, and a government-issued ID.

Run a Credit Check: Obtain written permission from the applicant to run a credit check. Review the credit report to assess the applicant's financial history, including credit score, debt-to-income ratio, and any past delinquencies or bankruptcies. Keep in mind that a lower credit score doesn't automatically disqualify an applicant, but it may necessitate additional considerations.

Check Rental History: Contact previous landlords to inquire about the applicant's rental history. Ask about their payment history, care of the property, and any lease violations or disputes. A tenant with a positive rental history is more likely to be a responsible and reliable tenant.

Verify Employment and Income: Verify the applicant's employment status and income. Ensure that their income is sufficient to cover the rent and living expenses comfortably. A common rule of thumb is that the tenant's monthly income should be at least three times the monthly rent.

Evaluate Criminal Background: Perform a criminal background check in compliance with local laws and regulations. While you must avoid discriminatory practices, it is essential to ensure the safety and well-being of other tenants and the property.

Conduct Interview and Reference Checks: Schedule an interview with potential tenants to assess their communication skills, demeanor, and compatibility with your property rules and policies. Contact personal references to gain insights into the applicant's character and reliability.

Section 2: Selecting Reliable and Responsible Tenants

Once you have completed the tenant screening process, it's time to make an informed decision and select tenants who demonstrate reliability, responsibility, and compatibility with your property.

Consistent Screening Criteria: Establish consistent screening criteria and apply them to all applicants to avoid any perception of discrimination. Having clear criteria will help you make objective decisions based on the applicants' qualifications.

Analyze Screening Results: Carefully review all the screening results and supporting documentation. Evaluate each applicant's qualifications based on factors such as rental history, creditworthiness, income, and background check results.

Trust Your Instincts: Trust your instincts about potential tenants. If something doesn't feel right or you have concerns, consider them carefully before making a final decision.

Communication with Applicants: Be transparent with applicants about the screening process and the reasons for your decision. If you decide not to accept an applicant, provide them with a clear explanation to maintain goodwill and avoid potential legal issues.

Leverage Technology: Utilize technology and online tools for tenant screening to streamline the process and access reliable information quickly. Many property management software platforms offer integrated tenant screening services.

Tenant Retention: Once you have selected reliable and responsible tenants, focus on tenant retention strategies to encourage them to renew their lease. Providing excellent customer service, addressing maintenance requests promptly, and maintaining open communication can foster long-term tenancy.

By implementing an effective tenant screening process and selecting reliable and responsible tenants, you can minimize potential risks and promote a positive rental experience for all parties involved. Thorough screening is an investment in the long-term success of your rental property, as it significantly contributes to a well-managed property with reliable and respectful tenants.

Chapter Nine: Crafting Lease Agreements and Rental Policies

Section 1: Creating Comprehensive Lease Contracts

Crafting a comprehensive lease agreement is of utmost importance when it comes to establishing a mutually beneficial and secure relationship between landlords and tenants. A well-crafted lease contract not only safeguards the rights and interests of both parties but also sets clear expectations for a harmonious tenancy. To create a robust and effective lease agreement, consider the following steps:

Seeking Legal Advice: Before drafting your lease agreement, it is prudent to consult with a knowledgeable real estate attorney who can offer valuable insights into local laws and regulations. Their expertise ensures that your lease is legally sound and tailored to your specific needs, protecting you from potential legal pitfalls.

Covering the Essentials: Start the lease agreement by providing vital information, such as the names of all involved parties, the property's complete address, the lease term's start and end dates, and the agreed-upon rent amount. Clearly state the rent payment schedule, acceptable methods of payment, and any penalties for late or missed payments.

Security Deposit Clauses: Address security deposits explicitly, stating the amount, how it will be held, the conditions for its use, and the process for refunding it upon lease termination. Transparency in this area can prevent misunderstandings and disputes later on, promoting a positive landlord-tenant relationship.

Maintenance and Repairs: Define the responsibilities of both parties concerning maintenance and repairs. Establish which tasks fall under the landlord's domain and which are the tenant's responsibility. Including a mechanism for reporting maintenance issues and a reasonable response timeframe can foster a well-maintained property and ensure timely resolution of maintenance concerns.

Addressing Property Use: Lay out specific guidelines on property usage, including rules about subletting, additional occupants, and pet policies. Clearly communicate any restrictions on smoking, alterations to the property, or activities not permitted on the premises. By setting clear guidelines, you establish a framework for responsible property use.

Termination and Renewal: Include clear provisions for lease termination and renewal. State the required notice period for both parties if they intend to renew or terminate the lease. Outline the conditions under which the lease can be terminated early, such as non-payment or breach of lease terms, providing a sense of security for both the landlord and the tenant.

Resolving Disputes: Consider including a dispute resolution clause, outlining the preferred method for resolving disagreements between the landlord and tenant. This clause can save both parties time and money by avoiding unnecessary legal battles and promoting open communication.

Section 2: Establishing Clear Rules and Policies

Transparent and well-communicated rental policies are essential for creating a positive and cooperative rental environment. When tenants understand their responsibilities and the property's guidelines, it leads to a more respectful and fulfilling tenancy. To establish clear rules and policies, consider the following strategies:

Tenant Handbook: Create a comprehensive tenant handbook that encompasses all the property's rules, policies, and procedures. Make it easily accessible to tenants, either in print or digitally. This handbook serves as a reference guide, fostering adherence to the property's guidelines and promoting a sense of community.

Noise and Quiet Hours: Set forth guidelines regarding noise levels, especially during designated quiet hours. Communicate community or building rules about noise and the consequences of violating them. Encourage respectful behavior to maintain a peaceful living environment for all tenants.

Parking and Vehicle Policies: Clearly outline parking policies, including designated parking spaces and any guest parking regulations. Specify the number of vehicles allowed per unit and provide information on proper parking procedures to ensure an organized and efficient parking system.

Pet Policies: If you allow pets on the property, establish comprehensive pet policies that cover breed and size restrictions, pet deposits, and rules for responsible pet ownership. This ensures a harmonious living environment for all tenants, including those with furry companions.

Tenant Responsibility for Utilities: Communicate which utilities the tenant is responsible for paying, such as electricity, water, gas, or internet services. This clarity helps tenants budget their expenses effectively and fosters a sense of responsibility for resource consumption.

Smoking Policy: If your property has a smoking policy, clearly state whether smoking is allowed or prohibited inside the rental units or on the property grounds. This promotes a healthier living environment and prevents potential conflicts between smoking and non-smoking tenants.

Tenant Responsibilities: Explicitly outline tenant responsibilities for maintaining cleanliness, proper waste disposal, and adherence to all property rules and regulations. This promotes a sense of accountability and respect among tenants, leading to a well-maintained and pleasant community.

Community Rules (if applicable): If the rental property is part of a community or homeowner's association, provide tenants with a copy of the community rules to ensure they understand their obligations as members of the community. Encourage participation and cooperation to foster a sense of belonging.

Communicate Policy Changes: Whenever changes are made to the lease agreement or rental policies during the tenancy, communicate these changes clearly in writing to all tenants with ample notice. Transparency about policy updates builds trust and cooperation, reducing the likelihood of misunderstandings.

Crafting lease agreements and establishing clear rental policies are essential elements of successful property management. By providing transparency, respecting tenants' needs, and promoting a harmonious living environment, you set the stage for a positive and gratifying rental experience for everyone involved. Regularly review and update your lease agreements and policies to ensure they remain current and align with any changes in local laws or regulations. Taking the time to create comprehensive agreements and policies demonstrates professionalism and dedication to providing a well-managed and desirable rental property.

Chapter Ten: Maintaining and Managing Rental Units

Section 1: Property Maintenance Best Practices

Effective property maintenance is essential for preserving the value of your rental units and ensuring a positive living experience for your tenants. Implementing best practices in property maintenance helps prevent costly repairs, reduces tenant complaints, and fosters tenant satisfaction.

Regular Inspections: Conduct routine inspections of the rental units and common areas. Regular inspections allow you to identify maintenance issues early on, addressing them before they escalate into more significant problems.

Preventative Maintenance: Create a preventive maintenance schedule to address potential issues before they occur. This includes tasks such as HVAC system maintenance, roof inspections, and pest control measures. Preventative maintenance can save both time and money by preventing major repairs in the long run.

Prompt Repairs: Address maintenance requests promptly and efficiently. Quick response times demonstrate your commitment to tenant satisfaction and can help build trust and goodwill with your tenants.

Quality Contractors: Hire reputable and skilled contractors for property maintenance and repairs. Vet contractors thoroughly and obtain multiple quotes for significant repairs to ensure fair pricing and quality workmanship.

Tenant Education: Educate tenants on their maintenance responsibilities, such as changing air filters, reporting leaks, and properly using appliances. Providing tenants with maintenance tips can contribute to the property's overall well-being and prolong the lifespan of appliances and fixtures.

Seasonal Maintenance: Adjust maintenance efforts based on seasonal needs. For instance, perform gutter cleaning in the fall and HVAC maintenance before the summer and winter seasons. Seasonal maintenance keeps the property in top condition throughout the year.

Landscaping and Curb Appeal: Maintain the property's exterior, including landscaping, lawn care, and curb appeal. A well-maintained exterior creates a positive impression and attracts quality tenants.

Document Maintenance: Keep detailed records of all maintenance and repairs performed on the property. Proper documentation helps with budgeting, tax purposes, and provides a historical record of property upkeep.

Section 2: Dealing with Repairs and Emergency Situations

Handling repairs and emergency situations efficiently is crucial for maintaining tenant satisfaction and ensuring their safety and well-being. Here are essential steps to manage repairs and emergencies effectively:

Emergency Contact Information: Provide tenants with emergency contact information, including a 24/7 emergency hotline and contact details for relevant service providers. Ensure tenants know how to report urgent issues outside of regular office hours.

Establish Protocols: Develop clear protocols for handling emergencies, such as floods, fires, or gas leaks. Ensure that all staff members, including property managers and maintenance personnel, are aware of the procedures and are trained to respond appropriately.

Prompt Communication: Respond to emergency maintenance requests immediately. Keep lines of communication open with tenants during emergencies, updating them on the status of the situation and any actions being taken.

Safety Precautions: Prioritize tenant safety during emergencies. If necessary, instruct tenants on evacuation procedures, the location of emergency exits, and how to shut off utilities in case of emergencies.

Vendor Relationships: Build strong relationships with reliable vendors and service providers who can respond quickly to emergency repair needs. Having trusted vendors on call ensures a swift resolution to critical situations.

Regular Maintenance Review: Review your property's maintenance needs regularly to identify potential problem areas. Being proactive can help prevent emergencies from arising and improve the overall condition of the rental units.

Tenant Communication: Encourage tenants to report maintenance issues promptly, even if they seem minor. Timely reporting allows for quick resolution and minimizes the risk of problems escalating.

Emergency Preparedness Training: Consider offering emergency preparedness training to your tenants, covering essential safety procedures and measures they can take during emergency situations.

Managing rental units requires a proactive approach to property maintenance and a well-thought-out strategy for dealing with repairs and emergencies. By implementing best practices in property maintenance and establishing clear protocols for handling emergencies, you can ensure the smooth operation of your rental property and maintain a positive relationship with your tenants. Remember that attentive property management leads to happy tenants and, in turn, contributes to the long-term success of your rental investment.

Chapter Eleven: Handling Tenant Issues and Disputes

Section 1: Conflict Resolution and Communication

Effective communication and conflict resolution are vital skills for landlords and property managers to maintain a harmonious relationship with tenants. Addressing tenant issues and disputes in a proactive and empathetic manner fosters tenant satisfaction and reduces the likelihood of conflicts escalating.

Active Listening: Practice active listening when tenants raise concerns or express grievances. Give them the opportunity to voice their issues fully and attentively. Demonstrating empathy and understanding can help de-escalate tensions and build trust.

Prompt Response: Respond to tenant issues promptly, even if it's just to acknowledge their concern initially. Prompt responses show that their concerns are taken seriously, and you are committed to finding a resolution.

Privacy and Confidentiality: Respect tenant privacy and confidentiality when handling sensitive matters. Avoid discussing tenant issues openly with other tenants or staff members.

Mediation: If conflicts arise between tenants, consider mediation as an alternative dispute resolution method. Mediation provides a neutral environment for all parties to discuss their concerns and work toward a mutually acceptable solution.

Written Communication: Whenever possible, communicate important matters in writing to maintain a record of discussions and agreements. Written communication helps avoid misunderstandings and provides evidence in case of future disputes.

Document Everything: Keep detailed records of all interactions with tenants, including maintenance requests, lease-related discussions, and dispute resolutions. Accurate documentation can be valuable evidence in case of legal disputes.

Follow Up: After addressing tenant issues or disputes, follow up with the tenants to ensure their concerns have been resolved to their satisfaction. A follow-up shows that you care about their well-being and are committed to maintaining a positive living experience.

Section 2: Dealing with Late Payments and Evictions

Late payments and evictions can be challenging situations for both landlords and tenants. While prevention is always preferable, knowing how to handle these situations professionally and legally is essential.

Clear Rent Collection Policies: Clearly outline rent collection policies in the lease agreement. State the due date, grace period (if any), and the consequences of late payments, such as late fees or other penalties.

Early Communication: If a tenant is unable to pay rent on time, encourage open communication. Discuss the reasons for the late payment and explore possible solutions, such as a temporary payment plan.

Late Payment Reminders: Send written reminders for late rent payments. A friendly reminder can be an effective way to prompt tenants to address the issue without resorting to harsher measures.

Late Fees: Enforce late fees according to the terms outlined in the lease agreement. Consistently apply late fees to ensure fairness and discourage late payments.

Eviction as a Last Resort: Eviction should be considered as a last resort when all other options have been exhausted. Follow the legal eviction process in your jurisdiction, and seek legal advice if necessary.

Serve Proper Notice: Comply with local laws regarding eviction notice periods. Serve proper written notice to the tenant, specifying the reason for eviction and the timeframe for vacating the property.

Professional Mediation: If facing difficult eviction situations, consider seeking mediation services to resolve the issue amicably and avoid costly legal battles.

Tenant Rights and Fair Housing: Always adhere to tenant rights and fair housing laws when dealing with late payments or eviction proceedings. Avoid discriminatory practices and treat all tenants fairly and equitably.

Handling tenant issues and disputes requires a patient and proactive approach. Effective communication, active listening, and understanding tenant perspectives are essential for resolving conflicts and maintaining positive relationships. When addressing late payments and eviction situations, always follow legal procedures and prioritize fairness and compliance with relevant laws. By fostering a respectful and supportive environment, you can create a positive living experience for your tenants and maintain the long-term success of your rental property.

Chapter Twelve: Building Positive Tenant Relationships

Section 1: Fostering Open Communication and Trust

Building positive tenant relationships is key to successful property management and long-term tenant retention. Fostering open communication and trust between landlords or property managers and tenants creates a supportive and respectful living environment.

Approachability: Be approachable and encourage open communication with tenants. Create an environment where tenants feel comfortable expressing their concerns, asking questions, and providing feedback.

Regular Check-Ins: Conduct periodic check-ins with tenants to ensure their needs are being met and to address any potential issues proactively. Regular communication shows that you care about their well-being and are attentive to their concerns.

Active Listening: Practice active listening when tenants share their thoughts or concerns. Give them your full attention and show empathy to better understand their perspectives and feelings.

Addressing Concerns Promptly: Respond to tenant concerns and maintenance requests promptly. Timely resolution of issues demonstrates your commitment to providing a positive living experience.

Transparency in Communication: Be transparent and honest in your communication with tenants. Clearly communicate any changes in property policies, rent rates, or upcoming maintenance work.

Respectful and Professional Communication: Maintain a professional and respectful tone in all communications with tenants.

Avoid confrontational language and address any conflicts with a solution-oriented approach.

Consider Tenant Feedback: Take tenant feedback seriously and consider implementing reasonable suggestions to improve the rental experience. Involving tenants in the decision-making process helps create a sense of ownership and belonging.

Section 2: Creating a Tenant-Centric Rental Experience

Providing a tenant-centric rental experience involves going beyond basic landlord responsibilities to ensure that tenants feel valued and cared for. Here are some strategies to create a tenant-centric approach:

Exceptional Customer Service: Provide exceptional customer service to tenants. Respond to their inquiries promptly and with a positive attitude, demonstrating your commitment to their satisfaction.

Tenant Appreciation: Show appreciation to tenants for their loyalty and cooperation. Consider hosting tenant appreciation events or providing small gestures of gratitude, such as holiday cards or small gifts.

Tenant Education: Educate tenants about their rights and responsibilities as well as property rules and policies. Empowering tenants with knowledge helps foster a sense of responsibility and encourages compliance.

Community Building: Encourage community building among tenants by organizing social events or creating shared spaces where they can interact and get to know one another. A sense of community can lead to a more pleasant living experience.

Personalized Approach: Whenever possible, personalize interactions with tenants based on their preferences and needs. This can include offering flexible lease terms or accommodating reasonable requests.

Proactive Maintenance: Implement preventive maintenance measures to address potential issues before they become major problems. Proactive maintenance demonstrates your commitment to tenant comfort and safety.

Regular Property Upgrades: Continuously improve the property by making upgrades and enhancements. Modernizing amenities or updating common areas can contribute to a more attractive and enjoyable living environment.

Consider Long-Term Tenants: Recognize and reward long-term tenants for their loyalty and reliability. Offer lease renewal incentives or consider keeping rent increases modest for tenants with a positive rental history.

By adopting a tenant-centric approach, you create a rental experience that fosters trust, satisfaction, and long-term tenant relationships. Prioritize open communication, active listening, and responsiveness to tenant needs to build a positive and respectful living environment. When tenants feel valued and appreciated, they are more likely to take pride in their rental unit and contribute to the overall well-being of the property. A tenant-centric approach not only benefits tenants but also enhances your reputation as a landlord and contributes to the success of your rental property in the long run.

Chapter Thirteen: Understanding Property Insurance

Section 1: Types of Insurance Coverage for Rental Properties

Having the appropriate insurance coverage for your rental property is essential to protect your investment and mitigate potential risks. Understanding the different types of insurance policies available for rental properties can help you make informed decisions about your insurance needs.

Property Insurance: Property insurance, also known as dwelling insurance or landlord insurance, covers the physical structure of the rental property from various perils, such as fire, theft, vandalism, and some natural disasters. It may also include coverage for other structures on the property, such as garages or sheds.

Liability Insurance: Liability insurance provides coverage for bodily injury or property damage claims that arise from accidents on your rental property. For example, if a tenant or guest is injured on the premises, liability insurance can help cover medical expenses and legal costs if you are found liable.

Loss of Rental Income Insurance: This type of insurance, also known as rental income protection, provides coverage for lost rental income if your rental property becomes uninhabitable due to a covered peril, such as a fire or storm damage. It helps compensate for the rental income you would have earned during the repair or rebuilding period.

Umbrella Insurance: Umbrella insurance is an additional liability coverage that goes beyond the limits of your primary liability insurance. It provides an extra layer of protection and can be beneficial if you want higher liability limits to safeguard your assets.

Flood Insurance: Standard property insurance typically does not cover flood damage. If your rental property is located in a flood-prone area, you may need to purchase a separate flood insurance policy through the National Flood Insurance Program (NFIP) or a private insurer.

Earthquake Insurance: Similarly, earthquake damage is usually not covered by standard property insurance. If your rental property is located in an earthquake-prone region, consider adding earthquake insurance to protect against such events.

Tenant Insurance: While not directly related to the landlord's insurance, it's essential to encourage your tenants to purchase renter's insurance. Tenant insurance covers their personal belongings and provides liability protection for any damages they may accidentally cause to the property.

Section 2: Mitigating Risks and Liabilities

As a landlord, you can take proactive steps to mitigate risks and liabilities associated with managing rental properties. By being diligent and implementing preventive measures, you can reduce the likelihood of accidents and potential liability issues.

Regular Property Inspections: Conduct regular inspections of your rental property to identify potential hazards or maintenance issues. Promptly address any safety concerns to minimize the risk of accidents.

Property Maintenance: Ensure that the property is well-maintained and meets all safety codes and standards. Keep walkways, staircases, and common areas free of hazards to prevent slips, trips, and falls.

Clear Lease Agreements: Draft comprehensive and clear lease agreements that outline tenant responsibilities and property rules. Clearly communicate safety guidelines to tenants to minimize the risk of accidents due to negligence.

Proper Screening of Tenants: Thoroughly screen potential tenants to identify those with a history of responsible behavior and good rental track records. A diligent tenant screening process can help avoid problematic tenants and reduce the risk of property damage.

Risk Management Plan: Develop a risk management plan that addresses potential hazards specific to your rental property. Implement preventive measures and safety protocols to reduce the likelihood of accidents and liabilities.

Emergency Preparedness: Have an emergency preparedness plan in place for handling potential crises, such as fires, floods, or severe weather events. Ensure that all tenants are aware of the emergency procedures and evacuation routes.

Security Measures: Implement security measures such as well-lit exteriors, secure locks on doors and windows, and possibly a security system to help deter criminal activities and ensure tenant safety.

Consult with Insurance Experts: Consult with insurance experts or insurance brokers to ensure you have the appropriate insurance coverage for your rental property. They can help you understand your options and tailor coverage to your specific needs.

By understanding the different types of insurance coverage available for rental properties and taking proactive steps to mitigate risks and liabilities, you can safeguard your investment and protect yourself from potential financial losses. A comprehensive approach to property insurance and risk management contributes to the long-term success of your rental business and provides peace of mind as a responsible landlord.

Chapter Fourteen: Taxation and Accounting for Landlords

Section 1: Tax Deductions and Reporting Income

As a landlord, understanding the taxation rules and maximizing tax deductions is essential for managing your rental property's finances effectively. Proper reporting of rental income and expenses is crucial for staying compliant with tax regulations. Here are some key considerations:

Rental Income Reporting: Report all rental income received from your tenants on your tax return. This includes rent payments, security deposits that are not intended to be forfeited, and any additional income from services or amenities provided to tenants.

Deductible Expenses: Familiarize yourself with deductible expenses related to your rental property. Common tax deductions for landlords include mortgage interest, property taxes, insurance premiums, property management fees, repairs, maintenance, utilities paid by the landlord, and depreciation.

Depreciation Deduction: Understand the concept of depreciation and how it applies to your rental property. Depreciation is a non-cash deduction that allows you to recover the cost of the property over its useful life. It can significantly reduce your taxable rental income.

Capital Improvements vs. Repairs: Differentiate between capital improvements and repairs for tax purposes. Capital improvements, which add value to the property or extend its useful life, are generally depreciated over time. Repairs, on the other hand, can be deducted in the current tax year.

Recordkeeping: Maintain detailed and organized records of all income and expenses related to your rental property. Good recordkeeping is essential for accurate tax reporting and can also be beneficial in case of tax audits.

Form 1099-MISC: If you make payments to independent contractors, such as maintenance workers or property managers, that total $600 or more during the tax year, you may need to issue them a Form 1099-MISC. Consult with a tax professional to ensure compliance with IRS reporting requirements.

State and Local Taxes: Be aware of state and local tax regulations that may apply to your rental property. Some areas impose additional taxes or fees on rental income, and compliance is crucial to avoid penalties.

Section 2: Working with Real Estate Accountants

Navigating the complexities of tax reporting and accounting for rental properties can be challenging. Seeking assistance from real estate accountants who specialize in landlord taxation can provide numerous benefits:

Expertise in Real Estate Taxation: Real estate accountants have in-depth knowledge of tax laws and regulations specific to rental properties. They can help you identify potential deductions, navigate tax credits, and stay up-to-date with any changes in tax laws that may impact your rental business.

Maximizing Deductions: A real estate accountant can advise you on maximizing tax deductions to reduce your taxable rental income. They can also help you properly categorize expenses and avoid common tax pitfalls.

Compliance and Audit Support: Working with an experienced real estate accountant can help ensure your tax returns are accurately filed and compliant with all tax laws. In case of a tax audit, they can provide valuable support and representation.

Entity Structuring: A real estate accountant can guide you in choosing the most advantageous business entity structure for your rental business. Different entities offer various tax benefits and liability protections.

Tax Planning Strategies: Real estate accountants can develop tax planning strategies tailored to your specific financial goals. They can assist with long-term tax planning to optimize your tax position and financial outcomes.

Financial Reporting: In addition to tax-related matters, real estate accountants can help you with financial reporting and analysis, offering insights into your rental property's financial health and performance.

Time and Cost Savings: By entrusting your tax and accounting needs to a professional, you can save time, reduce stress, and focus on other aspects of managing your rental property.

Working with real estate accountants is a wise investment for landlords who want to ensure accurate tax reporting, maximize deductions, and achieve overall financial efficiency. These professionals can be invaluable partners in managing your rental property's finances and safeguarding your long-term financial success as a landlord.

Chapter Fifteen: Scaling Your Rental Property Portfolio

Section 1: Expanding Investments and Diversifying

Once you have successfully managed a rental property and gained confidence in your abilities as a landlord, you may consider scaling your rental property portfolio to expand your real estate investments and diversify your holdings. Here are some strategies to help you achieve this:

Setting Clear Investment Goals: Define your long-term investment goals and develop a clear strategy to achieve them. Determine the number of properties you aim to acquire, the types of properties that align with your investment objectives, and the timeline for expanding your portfolio.

Financial Planning: Conduct a thorough financial analysis to understand your current financial position and how much capital you can allocate to new investments. Consider your risk tolerance, expected returns, and potential financing options to fund additional property acquisitions.

Market Research: Perform extensive market research to identify real estate markets with strong growth potential and rental demand. Look for areas with economic stability, job growth, population expansion, and favorable rental market conditions.

Property Analysis: Evaluate potential investment properties diligently. Analyze factors such as property location, rental income potential, maintenance costs, and property appreciation prospects. Perform a thorough due diligence process to assess the viability of each investment opportunity.

Financing Strategies: Explore different financing strategies to fund your property acquisitions. These may include traditional mortgages, private financing, partnerships, or real estate investment loans. Choose financing options that align with your investment goals and financial capacity.

Risk Management: As you scale your portfolio, consider diversifying your investments across various property types and locations. Diversification helps mitigate risks and reduces the impact of any individual property's performance on your overall portfolio.

Section 2: Managing Multiple Properties Efficiently

Managing multiple rental properties efficiently requires effective organization, time management, and systems to streamline operations. Here are strategies to help you manage multiple properties successfully:

Professional Property Management: As your portfolio grows, consider hiring a professional property management company to handle day-to-day operations. A property manager can handle tenant interactions, rent collection, property maintenance, and emergency issues on your behalf.

Standardized Processes: Develop standardized processes for rent collection, maintenance requests, and tenant screening. Having consistent procedures in place ensures that operations run smoothly and efficiently across all properties.

Utilize Technology: Implement property management software and tools to streamline administrative tasks, track expenses, and communicate with tenants. Technology can help automate repetitive processes and provide better visibility into your portfolio's performance.

Regular Inspections: Conduct regular inspections of all properties to identify maintenance needs and address issues proactively. A proactive approach to maintenance can save time and money in the long run.

Communication Channels: Establish efficient communication channels with tenants to address their concerns and respond promptly to inquiries. Clear and open communication fosters positive tenant relationships.

Financial Reporting: Maintain detailed financial records for each property and regularly review financial performance. Understanding the financial health of your properties allows you to make informed decisions and prioritize investments.

Leverage Resources: Utilize the expertise of real estate professionals, such as real estate agents, contractors, and accountants, to assist with various aspects of property management and maintenance.

Scaling your rental property portfolio requires careful planning, financial analysis, and effective property management strategies. By diversifying your investments, leveraging professional resources, and implementing efficient systems, you can successfully manage multiple properties and continue to grow your real estate portfolio with confidence. Regularly review and adjust your investment strategy to align with changing market conditions and your long-term investment objectives. With sound management practices and a commitment to continuous improvement, you can achieve your goals and build a thriving rental property portfolio.

Chapter Sixteen: Long-Term Wealth Building through Real Estate

Real estate investment offers unique opportunities for long-term wealth building, leveraging property appreciation, and building equity over time. As a savvy investor, you can use real estate as a vehicle for retirement planning and achieving financial freedom. Here's how:

Section 1: Leveraging Property Appreciation and Equity

Property Appreciation: Over time, real estate properties tend to appreciate in value, especially in growing markets. Property appreciation allows you to build wealth passively as your properties increase in value. Research and invest in markets with strong potential for property appreciation.

Forced Appreciation: Besides natural market appreciation, you can also engage in forced appreciation by improving the property's value through renovations and upgrades. Enhancing the property's features can lead to higher rental income and increased resale value.

Home Equity Growth: Paying down the mortgage on your rental properties builds equity. As you reduce your outstanding loan balance, your equity in the property increases. Home equity is an asset that can be leveraged for future investments or other financial goals.

1031 Exchange: Consider using a 1031 exchange to defer capital gains taxes when selling one investment property and purchasing another like-kind property. This strategy allows you to preserve your equity and continue building wealth through property acquisitions.

Refinancing: Refinancing your properties can provide access to additional funds by tapping into your accumulated equity. You can use these funds to invest in more properties or make improvements to existing ones, further boosting their value.

Section 2: Retirement Planning and Financial Freedom

Cash Flow and Passive Income: Rental properties generate consistent cash flow and passive income, which can be instrumental in funding your retirement. As you pay off mortgages and rental rates increase over time, your cash flow can grow significantly, supporting your retirement lifestyle.

Real Estate Portfolio Diversification: Diversifying your real estate portfolio with different property types and locations can provide stability and reduce risk. A well-diversified portfolio offers protection against fluctuations in specific markets or property sectors.

Long-Term Equity Building: Owning rental properties for the long term allows you to build substantial equity. When you eventually sell or refinance these properties, you can access this accumulated equity to fund your retirement or other financial goals.

Exit Strategy: Develop a well-thought-out exit strategy for your real estate investments. Determine when and how you plan to liquidate certain properties to realize their appreciation and convert them into retirement income.

Self-Directed IRA: Consider using a self-directed IRA (Individual Retirement Account) to invest in real estate. A self-directed IRA allows you to include real estate assets in your retirement savings, offering tax advantages and diversification.

Building a Real Estate Portfolio: Gradually build a diversified real estate portfolio with a mix of residential and commercial properties. Seek properties with solid growth potential and strong rental demand to ensure a steady stream of income during retirement.

Financial Planning: Consult with financial advisors and real estate professionals to develop a comprehensive retirement plan. A well-designed financial plan takes into account your real estate investments, other assets, and your retirement goals, helping you achieve financial freedom.

Long-term wealth building through real estate requires patience, strategic planning, and the ability to seize opportunities for growth. By leveraging property appreciation, building equity, and maintaining a carefully curated portfolio, you can create a path toward financial freedom and a secure retirement. Regularly review your investment strategy, stay informed about market trends, and adapt your plan as needed to maximize the potential of your real estate investments. With disciplined management and a focus on long-term objectives, real estate can be a powerful asset for building lasting wealth and securing your financial future.

Chapter Seventeen: Exploring Short-Term Rental Opportunities

Short-term rentals, such as vacation rentals and Airbnb properties, have become increasingly popular in the real estate market. They offer unique opportunities for investors, but they also come with distinct challenges. In this chapter, we will explore the pros and cons of short-term rentals and provide insights into effectively managing vacation and Airbnb properties.

Section 1: Pros and Cons of Short-Term Rentals

Pros of Short-Term Rentals:

a. Higher Rental Income: Short-term rentals often generate higher rental income compared to long-term rentals, especially during peak seasons and in popular tourist destinations.

b. Flexibility for Personal Use: With short-term rentals, property owners can use the property for personal vacations or family getaways when it's not booked by guests.

c. Seasonal Adjustments: Property owners can adjust rental rates seasonally to take advantage of high-demand periods and attract more guests.

d. Tax Benefits: Short-term rental owners may be eligible for certain tax deductions, similar to long-term rental properties, which can help reduce taxable income.

e. Opportunity for Appreciation: Properties located in desirable vacation destinations have the potential for appreciation over time, increasing the property's value.

Cons of Short-Term Rentals:

a. Vacancy Risk: Short-term rentals may experience higher vacancy rates, especially during off-peak seasons or economic downturns.

b. Higher Maintenance Costs: Frequent turnovers and guest usage can lead to higher maintenance and cleaning expenses.

c. Legal and Regulatory Considerations: Some cities and communities have strict regulations and zoning laws that restrict or regulate short-term rentals.

d. Time-Intensive Management: Managing short-term rentals can be more time-consuming due to frequent turnovers, guest communication, and marketing efforts.

e. Seasonal Fluctuations: Income from short-term rentals can vary significantly based on seasonal demand, making cash flow less predictable.

Section 2: Managing Vacation and Airbnb Properties

Professional Property Management: Consider hiring a professional property management company with experience in short-term rentals. They can handle guest bookings, communication, cleaning, and property maintenance.

High-Quality Listing: Create an attractive and informative listing with high-quality photographs that showcase the property's unique features and amenities.

Pricing Strategy: Develop a dynamic pricing strategy that considers seasonal demand, local events, and competitor rates. Adjust prices accordingly to maximize rental income.

Guest Screening: Implement a guest screening process to ensure that guests are reliable and respectful of the property. Platforms like Airbnb offer guest reviews that can help assess potential guests.

House Rules and Guidelines: Clearly communicate house rules and guidelines to guests before their stay to set expectations and prevent any issues during their visit.

Cleaning and Maintenance: Regularly inspect and clean the property between guest stays to maintain its condition and ensure a positive guest experience.

24/7 Support: Provide guests with 24/7 support to address any issues or emergencies promptly.

Legal Compliance: Familiarize yourself with local regulations and short-term rental laws. Ensure that your property is in compliance with all legal requirements.

Insurance Coverage: Review your insurance policy to ensure it covers short-term rentals and consider obtaining additional coverage for potential liabilities.

Short-term rentals offer an exciting opportunity for investors to maximize rental income and leverage unique property features. However, managing vacation and Airbnb properties requires careful planning, marketing efforts, and attention to guest satisfaction. By understanding the pros and cons and implementing effective management practices, you can optimize the success of your short-term rental venture and create a rewarding investment experience.

Chapter Eighteen: Incorporating Sustainable Practices

In recent years, there has been a growing emphasis on sustainability and eco-friendly practices in the real estate industry. As a landlord, adopting sustainable practices in your rental properties not only benefits the environment but can also attract environmentally-conscious tenants. This chapter explores eco-friendly upgrades for rental properties and strategies for appealing to tenants who prioritize sustainable living.

Section 1: Eco-Friendly Upgrades for Rental Properties

Energy-Efficient Appliances: Replace outdated appliances with energy-efficient models, such as ENERGY STAR-rated refrigerators, dishwashers, and washing machines. Energy-efficient appliances reduce utility costs and appeal to eco-conscious tenants.

LED Lighting: Upgrade all light fixtures to LED bulbs, which consume significantly less energy and have a longer lifespan compared to traditional incandescent bulbs.

Smart Thermostats: Install smart thermostats that allow tenants to program and control heating and cooling systems efficiently. These devices can lead to energy savings and provide more comfortable living conditions.

Low-Flow Fixtures: Replace standard faucets, showerheads, and toilets with low-flow alternatives to conserve water usage without compromising on performance.

Renewable Energy Sources: Consider installing solar panels on the property to generate renewable energy and reduce dependency on traditional electricity sources.

Insulation Improvements: Enhance insulation in the property to improve energy efficiency and reduce heating and cooling costs.

Sustainable Flooring: Choose eco-friendly flooring options, such as bamboo, cork, or recycled materials, which are more sustainable than traditional flooring materials.

Rainwater Harvesting: Implement rainwater harvesting systems to collect and reuse rainwater for irrigation and other non-potable water needs.

Section 2: Attracting Environmentally Conscious Tenants

Green Marketing: Highlight the eco-friendly features and upgrades of your rental property in your marketing materials and listings. Use green keywords and eco-friendly certifications to attract environmentally conscious tenants.

Eco-Friendly Community: Emphasize any nearby eco-friendly amenities, such as parks, nature trails, public transportation, or recycling centers, that make your property appealing to tenants looking for a sustainable lifestyle.

Green Certification: Obtain green certifications, such as LEED (Leadership in Energy and Environmental Design) or Energy Star, for your rental property. Green certifications enhance your property's credibility as an environmentally-friendly option.

Recycling and Waste Management: Provide convenient recycling options and educate tenants about waste reduction practices to encourage sustainable behavior.

Sustainable Landscaping: Create a sustainable landscape with native plants, drought-resistant species, and efficient irrigation systems to minimize water usage and maintenance needs.

Green Incentives: Offer green incentives to tenants who practice sustainable living, such as a discount on rent for using renewable energy or water-saving practices.

Green Lease Addendum: Consider adding a green lease addendum that encourages tenants to adopt sustainable practices during their tenancy.

Tenant Education: Provide resources and educational materials on sustainable living practices to help tenants understand how they can contribute to a greener lifestyle.

By incorporating sustainable practices and eco-friendly upgrades in your rental properties, you can reduce environmental impact, attract environmentally-conscious tenants, and differentiate your properties in the competitive rental market. Emphasizing the benefits of sustainable living and offering eco-friendly amenities can be a compelling selling point for potential tenants who value environmental responsibility and are seeking rental properties that align with their values.

Chapter Nineteen: Exiting Your Rental Property Investment

At some point, real estate investors may decide to exit their rental property investment for various reasons, such as capitalizing on appreciation, diversifying their portfolio, or pursuing other opportunities. This chapter explores strategies for selling or 1031 exchanging rental properties and how to evaluate the market to determine the optimal timing for your exit.

Section 1: Strategies for Selling or 1031 Exchanging

Selling Your Rental Property:

a. Market Analysis: Conduct a comprehensive market analysis to determine the current value of your rental property. Consider factors such as recent comparable sales, local real estate trends, and economic indicators.

b. Repairs and Improvements: Address any necessary repairs or improvements to enhance the property's appeal and maximize its resale value.

c. Marketing: Develop a targeted marketing plan to attract potential buyers. Utilize various channels, such as online listings, social media, and real estate agents, to reach a broad audience.

d. Pricing Strategy: Set a competitive and realistic listing price based on the market analysis. Overpricing can lead to a longer time on the market, while underpricing may result in missed opportunities.

e. Negotiation and Closing: Be prepared to negotiate with potential buyers and be flexible in reaching a mutually beneficial agreement. Work with a real estate agent or attorney to navigate the closing process smoothly.

1031 Exchange:

a. Understand the Process: Familiarize yourself with the rules and requirements of a 1031 exchange, which allows you to defer capital gains taxes by reinvesting the proceeds from the sale of one rental property into a like-kind replacement property.

b. Identify Replacement Properties: Identify potential replacement properties that meet the criteria for a 1031 exchange. You have a limited timeframe to identify these properties after selling your original rental property.

c. Qualified Intermediary: Work with a qualified intermediary, also known as a facilitator or accommodator, to handle the exchange process and ensure compliance with IRS regulations.

d. Timelines: Comply with strict timelines for completing the 1031 exchange, including the identification period and the exchange period, to avoid disqualifying the exchange for tax deferral.

Section 2: Evaluating the Market for Timing Your Exit

Economic Conditions: Monitor economic indicators, such as interest rates, employment rates, and GDP growth, to gauge the overall health of the real estate market.

Local Real Estate Trends: Study local real estate trends and consider factors like inventory levels, days on market, and price changes in your specific market.

Rental Demand: Assess the demand for rental properties in your area. High rental demand can indicate a robust market for selling your property to investors or owner-occupants.

Property Appreciation: Evaluate the historical and projected property appreciation in your area. Selling during a period of significant appreciation can maximize your return on investment.

Portfolio Diversification: Consider your overall investment portfolio and whether diversifying into other asset classes or geographic locations aligns with your long-term financial goals.

Personal Financial Goals: Evaluate how the sale or exchange of your rental property aligns with your personal financial goals and investment strategy.

Tax Implications: Consult with a tax professional to understand the tax implications of selling or exchanging your rental property and how it fits into your broader tax planning.

Exiting your rental property investment requires careful consideration of market conditions, your investment objectives, and potential tax implications. Whether you decide to sell your property outright or pursue a 1031 exchange, timing and strategic planning can play a crucial role in achieving your desired outcomes. By conducting thorough market research and seeking professional guidance, you can confidently make informed decisions regarding the best course of action for exiting your rental property investment.

Chapter Twenty: The Future of Real Estate Investing

As the real estate industry evolves, rental property management is experiencing significant changes driven by technology advancements and shifting market trends. This chapter explores the emerging trends and innovations in rental property management and highlights the importance of embracing technology and market shifts for continued success in real estate investing.

Section 1: Trends and Innovations in Rental Property Management

Smart Home Technology: The integration of smart home technology is becoming increasingly popular in rental properties. Landlords can install smart thermostats, keyless entry systems, and smart security cameras, allowing for remote monitoring and energy efficiency.

PropTech Solutions: Property technology, or PropTech, offers innovative solutions for property management tasks. Cloud-based software, virtual tours, online rent payments, and automated communication systems streamline operations and enhance tenant experience.

Tenant Experience: The focus on tenant experience is gaining momentum. Landlords are prioritizing tenant satisfaction, offering amenities like coworking spaces, fitness centers, and community events to attract and retain high-quality tenants.

Sustainable and Green Buildings: Environmentally-conscious tenants are seeking eco-friendly rental properties with sustainable features like solar panels, rainwater harvesting systems, and energy-efficient appliances.

Co-Living Spaces: Co-living spaces, where tenants share common areas and amenities, are gaining popularity among younger generations who value community and affordability.

Short-Term Rentals: The short-term rental market, including vacation rentals and Airbnb properties, continues to grow as travelers seek unique and personalized experiences.

Section 2: Embracing Technology and Market Shifts

Adapting to Virtual Trends: Embrace virtual property tours, online tenant screenings, and virtual property management to meet the changing preferences of tech-savvy renters.

Data-Driven Decision Making: Utilize data analytics to assess market trends, rental demand, and property performance. Data-driven insights can inform investment decisions and improve operational efficiency.

Tenant Communication: Embrace digital communication channels to maintain strong tenant relationships and promptly address inquiries and concerns.

Proactive Maintenance: Utilize property management software to schedule and track maintenance tasks proactively, ensuring the property remains in top condition.

ESG Investing: Consider environmental, social, and governance (ESG) factors in real estate investment decisions. ESG considerations are gaining importance among investors and tenants alike.

Market Research: Continuously monitor market trends and shifts to identify emerging opportunities and adapt your investment strategy accordingly.

Property Security: Embrace advanced security systems and protocols to ensure the safety of your properties and the well-being of your tenants.

Continuous Learning: Stay informed about the latest advancements in real estate technology and industry best practices through ongoing education and networking.

In conclusion, the future of real estate investing lies in embracing technology, understanding market shifts, and catering to the preferences of modern tenants. As rental property management evolves, investors who adapt to the latest trends and leverage innovative tools will be better positioned for success. By incorporating smart home technology, PropTech solutions, and sustainable practices, landlords can enhance tenant experience and attract quality tenants. Continuous learning and a forward-thinking mindset are essential for thriving in the dynamic and ever-evolving world of real estate investing.

The world of real estate investing is constantly evolving, driven by technological advancements, changing market trends, and shifting tenant preferences. As we have explored in this book, effective rental property management requires a comprehensive understanding of various aspects, from setting realistic investment goals to embracing sustainable practices and leveraging the power of technology. Through careful planning, proactive decision-making, and a focus on tenant satisfaction, real estate investors can build a successful and profitable rental property portfolio.

Incorporating sustainable practices in rental properties not only benefits the environment but also attracts environmentally-conscious tenants. Energy-efficient upgrades, renewable energy sources, and eco-friendly landscaping can reduce the property's ecological footprint while appealing to tenants who prioritize sustainable living.

Embracing technology is crucial for staying competitive in the rental property market. PropTech solutions, smart home technology, and data-driven decision-making streamline property management tasks, improve tenant experiences, and enhance overall operational efficiency.

As the rental market continues to evolve, short-term rentals, co-living spaces, and the emphasis on tenant experience are shaping the future of real estate investing. Adapting to virtual trends, implementing proactive maintenance strategies, and prioritizing property security are essential for meeting the evolving needs and expectations of modern tenants.

Throughout this book, we have explored various aspects of real estate investing and rental property management, from initial research and property acquisition to sustainable practices and embracing technology. Successful landlords are those who remain agile, continuously learning, and staying ahead of market shifts.

The journey of managing rental properties can be both rewarding and challenging. By setting clear investment goals, fostering positive tenant relationships, and making data-driven decisions, investors can achieve long-term wealth building and financial freedom through their real estate ventures.

As you embark on your real estate investment journey, remember to stay informed, seek professional guidance when needed, and adapt your strategies to capitalize on emerging trends. With dedication, perseverance, and a commitment to excellence, you can build a thriving rental property portfolio and create a successful future in real estate investing.

Thank you.